CALIFORNIA
NATIVE AMERICAN TRIBES

WINTU TRIBE

© 92 Liddell

by

Mary Null Boulé

Book Twenty-two in a series of twenty-six

Dear Reader,

You will find an outline of this chapter's important topics at the back of the booklet. It is there for you to use in writing a report or giving an oral report on this tribe.

If you first read the booklet completely, then you can use the outline as a guide to write your report in your own words, instead of copying sentences from the chapter.

Good luck, read carefully,
and use your own words.

MNB

TWENTY-SEVEN

CALIFORNIA NATIVE AMERICAN TRIBES

WINTU TRIBE

by
Mary Null Boulé

Illustrated by
Daniel Liddell

Merryant Publishing
Vashon, Washington

Book Number Twenty-two in a series of twenty-six

This series is dedicated to Virginia Harding, whose editing expertise and friendship brought this project to fruition.

Library of Congress Catalog Card Number: 92-61897

ISBN: 1-877599-44-1

Copyright © 1992, Merryant Publishing

7615 S.W. 257th St., Vashon, WA 98070.

FOREWORD

Native American people of the United States are often living their lives away from major cities and away from what we call the mainstream of life. It is, then, interesting to learn of the important part these remote tribal members play in our everyday lives.

More than 60% of our foods come from the ancient Native American's diet. Farming methods of today also can be traced back to how tribal women grew crops of corn and grain. Many of our present day ideas of democracy have been taken from tribal governments. Even some 1,500 Native American words are found in our English language today.

Fur traders bought furs from tribal hunters for small amounts of money, sold them to Europeans and Asians for a great deal of money, and became rich. Using their money to buy land and to build office buildings, some traders started business corporations which are now the base of our country's economy.

There has never been enough credit given to these early Americans who took such good care of our country when it was still in their care. The time has come to realize tribal contributions to our society today and to give Native Americans not only the credit, but the respect due them.

Mary Boulé

A-frame cradle for girls; tule matting. Tubatulabal tribe.

GENERAL INFORMATION

Out of Asia, many thousands of years ago, came Wanderers. Some historians think they were the first people to set foot on our western hemisphere. These Wanderers had walked, step by step, onto our part of the earth while hunting and gathering food. They probably never even knew they had moved from one continent to another as they made their way across a land bridge, a narrow strip of land between Siberia and what is now Russia, and the state of Alaska.

Historians do not know exactly how long ago the Wanderers might have crossed the land bridge. Some of them say 35,000 years ago. What historians do know is that these people slowly moved down onto land that we now call the United States of America. Today it would be very hard to follow their footsteps, for the land bridge has been covered with sea water since the thawing of the ice age.

Those Wanderers who made their way to California were very lucky, indeed. California was a land with good weather most of the year and was filled with plenty of plant and animal foods for them to eat.

The Wanderers who became California's Native Americans did not organize into large tribes like the rest of the North American tribes. Instead, they divided into groups, or tribelets, sometimes having as many as 250 people. A tribelet could number as few as three, to as many as thirty villages located close to each other. Some tribelets had only one chief, a leader who lived in the largest village. Many tribes had a chief for each village. Some leaders had no real power but were thought to be wise. Tribal members always listened with respect to what their chief had to say.

From 20 to 100 people could be living in one village, which usually had several houses. In most cases, these groups of people were related to each other. From five to ten people of one family lived in one house. For instance, a mother, a father, two or three children, a grandmother, or aunt or daughter-in-law might live together.

Village members together would own the land important to them for their well-being. Their land might include oak trees with precious acorns, streams and rivers, and plants which were good to eat. Streams and rivers were especially important to a tribe's quality of life. Water drew animals to it; that meant more food for the tribe to eat. Fish were a good source of food, and traveling by boat was often easier than walking long distances. Water was needed in every part of tribal life.

Village and tribelet land was carefully guarded. Each group knew exactly where the boundaries of its land were found. Boundaries were known by landmarks such as mountains or rivers, or they might also be marked by poles planted in the ground. Some boundary lines were marked by rocks, or by objects placed there by tribal members. The size of a territory had to be large enough to supply food to every person living there.

The California tribes spoke many languages. Sometimes villages close together even had a problem understanding one another. This meant that each group had to be sure of the boundaries of other tribes around them when gathering food. It would not be wise to go against the boundaries and the customs of neighbors. The Native Americans found if they respected the boundaries of their neighbors, not so many wars had to be fought. California tribes, in spite of all their differences, were not as warlike as other tribes in our country.

Not only did the California tribes speak different languages, but their members also differed in size. Some tribes were very tall, almost six feet tall. The shortest people came from the Yuki tribe which had territory in what is now Mendocino County. They measured only about 5'2" tall. All Native Americans, regardless of size, had strong, straight black hair and dark brown eyes.

TRADE

Trading between tribes was an important part of life. Inland tribes had large animal hides that coastal tribes wanted. By trading the hides to coastal groups, inland tribes would receive fish and shells, which they in turn wanted. Coastal tribes also wanted minerals and rocks mined in the mountains by inland tribes. Obsidian rock from the northern mountains was especially wanted for arrowheads. There were, as well, several minerals, mined in the inland mountains, which could be made into the colorful body paints needed for religious ceremonies.

Southern tribes particularly wanted steatite from the Gabrielino tribe. Steatite, or soapstone, was a special metal which allowed heat to spread evenly through it. This made it a good choice to be used for cooking pots and flat frying pans. It could be carved into bowls because of its softness and could be decorated by carving designs into it. Steatite came from Catalina Island in the Coastal Gabrielino territory. Gabrielinos found steatite to be a fine trading item to offer for the acorns, deerskins, or obsidian stone they needed.

When people had no items to trade but needed something, they used small strings of shells for money. The small dentalium shells, which came from the far distant Northwest coast, had great value. Strings of dentalia usually served as money in the Northern California tribes, although some dentalia was used in the Central California tribes.

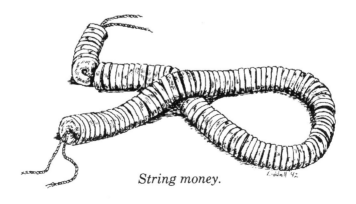

String money.

6

In southern California clam shells were broken and holes were bored through the center of each piece. Then the pieces were rounded and polished with sandstone and strung into strings for money. These were not thought to be as valuable as dentalia.

Strings of shell money were measured by tattoo marks on the trader's lower arm or hand.

Here is a sample of shell value:

> A house, three strings
> A fishing place, one to three strings
> Land with acorn-bearing oak trees, one to five strings

A great deal of rock and stone was traded among the tribes for making tools. Arrows had to have sharp-edged stone for tips. The best stone for arrow tips was obsidian (volcanic glass) because, when hit properly, it broke off into flakes with very sharp edges. California tribes considered obsidian to be the most valuable rock for trading.

Some tribes had craftsmen who made knives with wooden handles and obsidian blades. Often the handles were decorated with carvings. Such knives were good for trading purposes. Stone mortars and pestles, used by the women for grinding grains into flour, were good trading items.

BASKETS & POTTERY

California tribal women made beautiful baskets. The Pomo and Chumash baskets, what few are left, show us that the women of those tribes might have been some of the finest basketmakers in the world. Baskets were used for gathering and storing food, for carrying babies, and even for hauling water. In emergencies, such as flooding waters, sometimes children, women, and tribal belongings crossed the swollen rivers and streams in huge, woven baskets! Baskets were so tightly woven that not a drop of water could leak from them.

Baskets also made fine cooking pots. Very hot rocks were taken from a fire and tossed around inside baskets with a looped tree branch until food in the basket was cooked.

Most baskets were made to do a certain job, but some baskets were designed for their beauty alone and were excellent for trading. Older women of a tribe would teach young girls how to weave baskets.

Pottery was not used by many California tribes. What little there was seems to have been made by those tribes living near to the Navaho and Mohave tribes of Arizona, and it shows their style. For example, pottery of the California tribes did not have much decoration and was usually a dull red color. Designs were few and always in yellow.

Ohlone hunter wearing deerskin camouflage.

Long thin coils of clay were laid one on top the other. Then the coils were smoothed between a wooden paddle and a small stone to shape the bowl. Pottery from California Native Americans has been described as light weight and brittle (easily broken), probably because of the kind of clay soil found in California.

HUNTING & FISHING

Tribal men spent much of their time making hunting and fishing tools. Bows and arrows were built with great care, to make them shoot as accurately as possible. Carelessly made hunting weapons caused fewer animals to be killed and people then had less food to eat.

Bows made by men of Southern California tribes were made long and narrow. In the northern part of the state bows were a little shorter, thinner, and wider than those of their northern neighbors. Size and thickness of bows depended on the size trees growing in a tribe's territory. The strongest bows were wrapped with sinew, the name given to animal tendons. Sinew is strong and elastic like a rubber band.

Arrows were made in many sizes and shapes, depending on their use. For hunting larger animals, a two-piece arrow was used. The front piece of the arrow shaft was made so that it would remain in the animal, even if the back part was removed or broken off. The arrowhead, or point, was wrapped to the front piece of the shaft. This kind of arrow was also used in wars.

Young boys used a simple wooden arrow with the end sharpened to a point. With this they could hunt small animals like birds and rabbits. The older men of the tribe taught boys how to make their own arrows, how to aim properly, and how to repair broken weapons.

Tribal men spent many hours making and mending fishing nets. The string used in making nets often came from the fibers of plants. These fibers were twisted to make them strong and tough, then knotted into netting. Fences, or weirs, that had one small opening for fish, were built across streams. As the fish swam through the opening they would be caught in netting or harpooned by a waiting fisherman.

Hooks, if used at all, were cut from shells. Mostly hooks could be found when the men fished in large lakes or when catching trout in high mountain areas. Hooks were attached to heavy plant fiber string.

Dip nets, made of netting attached to branches that were bent into a circle, were used to catch fish swimming near shore. Dip nets had long handles so the fishermen could reach deep into the water.

Sometimes a mild poison was placed on the surface of shallow water. This confused the fish and caused them to float to the surface of the water, where they could be scooped up by a waiting fisherman. Not enough poison was used to make humans ill.

Not all fishing was done from the shore. California tribes used two kinds of boats when fishing. Canoes, dug out of one half a log, were useful for river fishing. These were square at each end, round on the bottom, and very heavy. Some of them were well-finished, often even having a carved seat in them.

Today we think of "balsa" as a very lightweight wood, but in Spanish, the word balsa means "raft". That is why Spanish explorers called the Native American canoes, made from tule reeds, "balsa" boats.

Balsa boats were made of bundled tule reeds and were used throughout most of California. They made into safe, lightweight boats for lake and river use. Usually the balsa canoe had a long, tightly tied bundle of tule for the boat bottom and one bundle for each side of the canoe. The front of the canoe was higher than the back. Balsa boats could be steered with a pole or with a paddle, like a raft.

Men did most of the fishing, women were in charge of gathering grasses, seeds, and acorns for food. After the food was collected, it was either eaten right away or made ready for winter storage.

Except for a few southern groups, California tribes had permanent villages where they lived most of the year. They also had food-gathering places they returned to each year to collect acorns, salt, fish, and other foods not found near their villages.

FOOD

Many different kinds of plant food grew wild in California in the days before white people arrived. Berries and other plant foods grew in the mountains. Forests offered the local tribes everything from pine nuts to animals.

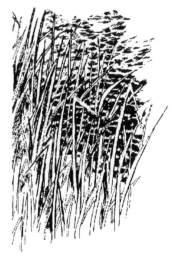

Native Americans found streams full of fish for much of the year. Inland fresh water lakes had large tule reeds growing along their shores. Tule could be eaten as food when plants were young and tender. More important, however, tule was used in making fabric for clothes and for building boats and houses. Tule was probably the most useful plant the California Native Americans found growing wild in their land.

Like all deserts, the one in southern California had little water or fish, but small animals and cactus plants made good food for the local tribes. They moved from place to place harvesting whatever was ripe. Tribal members always knew when and where to find the best food in their territory.

Acorns were the main source of food for all California tribes. Acorn flour was as important to the California Native Americans as wheat is to us today. Five types of California oak trees produced acorns that could be eaten. Those from black oak and tanbark oak seem to have been the favorite kinds.

Since some acorns tasted better than others, the tastiest ones were collected first. If harvest of the favorite acorn was poor some years, then less tasty acorns had to be eaten all winter long.

So important were acorns to California Indians that most tribes built their entire year around them. Acorn harvest marked the beginning of their calendar year. Winter was counted as so many months after acorn harvest, and summer was counted by the number of months before the next acorn harvest.

Acorn harvest ceremonies usually were the biggest events of the year. Most celebrations took place in mid-October and included dancing, feasts, games of chance, and reunions with relatives. Harvest festivals lasted for many days. They were a time of joy for everyone.

The annual acorn gathering lasted two to three weeks. Young boys climbed the oak trees to shake branches; some men used long poles to knock acorns to the ground. Women loaded the nuts into large cone-shaped burden baskets and carried them to a central place where they were put in the sun to dry.

Once the acorns were dried, the women carried them back to the tribe's permanent villages. There they lined special basket-like storage granaries with strong herbs to keep insects away, then stored the acorns inside. Granaries were placed on stilts to keep animals from getting into them and were kept beside tribal houses.

Preparing acorns for each meal was also the women's job. Shells were peeled by hitting the acorns with a stone hammer on an anvil (flat) stone. Meat from the nut was then laid on a stone mortar. A mortar was usually a large stone with a slight dip on its surface. Sometimes the mortar had a bottomless basket, called a hopper, glued to its top. This kept the acorn meat from sliding off the mortar as it was beaten. The meat was then pounded with a long stone pestle. Acorn flour was scraped away from the hopper's sides with a soaproot fiber brush during this process.

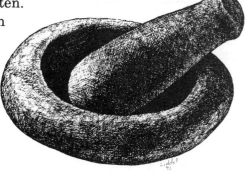

From there the flour was put into an open-worked basket and sifted. A fine flour came through the bottom of the basket, while the larger pieces were put back in the mortar for more pounding.

The most important process came after the acorn flour was sifted. Acorn flour has a very bitter-tasting tannin in it. This bitter taste was removed by a method called leaching. Many tribes leached the flour by first scooping out a hollow in sand near water. The hollow was lined with leaves to keep the flour from washing away. A great deal of hot water was poured through the flour to wash out (leach) the bitterness. Sometimes the flour was put into a basket for the leaching process, instead of using sand and leaves.

Finally the acorn flour was ready to be cooked. To make mush, heated stones were placed in the basket with the flour. A looped tree branch or two long sticks were used to toss the hot rocks around so the basket would not burn. When the mush had boiled, it could be eaten. If the flour and water mixture was baked in an earthen oven, it became a kind of bread. Early explorers wrote that it was very tasty.

Historians have estimated that one family would eat from 1500 to 2000 pounds of acorn flour a year. One reason California native Americans did not have to plant seeds and raise crops was because there were so many acorns for them to harvest each year.

Whether they ate fish or shellfish or plant food or animal meat, nature supplied more than enough food for the Native Americans who lived in California long ago. Many believed their good fortune in having fine weather and plenty to eat came from being good to their gods.

RELIGION

Tribal members had strong beliefs in the power of spirits or gods around them. Each tribe was different, but all felt the importance of never making a spirit angry with them. For that reason a celebration to thank the spirit-gods for treating them well, took place before each food gathering and before each hunting trip, and after each food harvest.

Usually spiritual powers were thought to belong to birds or animals. Most California tribespeople felt bears were very wicked and should not be eaten. But Coyote seems to have been a kind leader who helped them if they were in trouble, even though he seems to have been a bit naughty at times. Eagle was thought to be very powerful and good to native Americans. In some tribes, Eagle was almost as powerful as Sun.

Tribes placed importance on different gods, according to the tribe's needs. Rain gods were the most important spirits to desert tribes. Weather gods, who might bring less rain or warmer temperatures, were important to northern tribes. A great many groups felt there were gods for each of the winds: North, South, East and West. The four directions were usually included in their ceremonial dances and were used as part of the decorations on baskets, pots, and even tools.

Animals were not only worshipped and believed to be spirit-gods, like Deer or Antelope, but tribal members felt there was a personal animal guardian for each one of them. If a tribal member had a deer as guardian, then that person could never kill a deer or eat deer meat.

California Native Americans believed in life after death. This made them very respectful of death and very fearful of angering a dead person. Once someone died, the name of the dead person could never again be said aloud. Since it was easy to accidentally say a name aloud, the name was usually given to a new baby. Then the dead person would not become angry.

Shamans were thought to be the keepers of religious beliefs and to have the ability to talk directly to spirit-gods. It was the job of a village shaman to cure sick people, and to speak to the gods about the needs of the people. Some tribes had several kinds of shamans in one village. One shaman did curing, one scared off evil spirits, while another took care of hunters.

Not all shamans were nice, so people greatly feared their power. However, if shamans had no luck curing sick people or did not bring good luck in hunting, the people could kill them. Most shamans were men, but in a few tribes, women were doctors.

Most California tribal myths have been lost to history because they were spoken and never written down. The legends were told and retold on winter nights around the home fires. Sadly, these were forgotten after the missionaries brought Christianity to California and moved tribal members into the missions.

A few stories still remain, however. It is thought by historians that northwest California tribes were the only ones not to have a myth on how they were created. They did not feel that the world was made and prepared for human beings. Instead, their few remaining stories usually tell of mountain peaks or rivers in their own territory.

The central California tribes had creation stories of a great flood where there was only water on earth. They tell of how man was made from a bit of mud that a turtle brought up from the bottom of the water.

Many southwest tribes believed there was a time of no sky or water. They told of two clouds appearing which finally became Sky and Earth.

Throughout California, however, all tribes had myths that told of Eagle as the leader, Coyote as chief assistant, and of less powerful spirits like Falcon or Hawk.

Costumes for religious ceremonies often imitated these animals they worshipped or feared. Much time was spent in making the dance costumes as beautiful as possible. Red woodpecker feathers were so brilliant a color they were used to decorate religious headdresses, necklaces, or belts. Deerskin clothing was fringed so shell beads could be attached to each thin strip of leather.

Eagle feathers were felt to be the most sacred of religious objects. Sometimes they were made into whole robes.

Religious feather charm.

Usually, though, the feathers were used just for decorations. All these costumes were valuable to the people of each tribe. The village chief was in charge of taking care of the costumes, and there was terrible punishment for stealing them. Clothing worn everyday was not fancy like costuming for rituals.

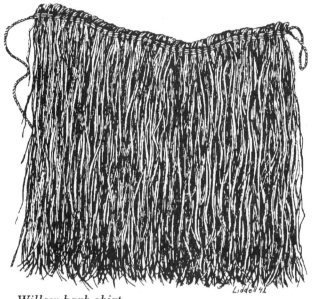

Willow bark skirt.

CLOTHING

Central and southern California's fine weather made regular clothes not really very important to the Native Americans. The children and men went naked most of the year, but most women wore a short apron-like skirt. These skirts were usually made in two pieces, front and back aprons, with fringes cut into the bottom edges. Often the skirt was made from the inner bark of trees, shredded and gathered on a cord. Sometimes the skirt was made from tule or grass.

In northern California and in rainy or windy weather elsewhere in the state, animal-skin blankets were worn by both men and women. They were used like a cape and wrapped around the body. Sometimes the cape was put over one shoulder and under the other arm, then tied in front. All kinds of skins were used; deer, otter, wildcat, but sea-otter fur was thought to be the best. If the skin was from a small animal, it was cut into strips and woven together into a fabric. At night the cape became a blanket to keep the person warm.

Because of the rainy weather in northern California, the women wore basket caps all the time. Women of the central and south tribes wore caps only when carrying heavy loads, where the forehead had to be used as support. Then a cap helped keep too much weight from being placed on the forehead.

Most California people went barefoot in their villages. For journeys into rough land, going to war, wood gathering, or in colder weather, the tribesmen in central and northwest California wore a one-piece soft shoe with no extra sole, which went high up on the leg.

Southern California tribespeople, however, wore sandals most of the time, wearing high, soled moccasins only when they traveled long distances or into the mountains. Leggings of skin were worn in snow, and moccasins were sometimes lined with grass for more comfort and warmth.

VILLAGE LIFE

Houses of the California tribes were made of materials found in their area. Usually they were round with domed roofs. Except for a few tribes, a house floor was dug into the earth a few feet. This was wise, for it made the home warmer in winter and cooler in summer. It also meant that less material was needed to make house walls.

Framework for the walls was made from bendable branches tied to support poles. Some frames of the houses were covered with earth and grass. Others were covered with large slabs of redwood or pine bark. Central California

Split-stick clapper, rhythm instrument. Hupa tribe.

villagers made large woven mats of tule reed to cover the tops and sides of houses. In the warmer southern area, brush and smaller pieces of bark were used for house walls.

Most California Native American villages had a building called a sweathouse, where the men could be found when they were not hunting, fishing or traveling. It was a very important place for the men, who used it rather like a clubhouse. They could sweat and then scrape themselves clean with curved ribs of deer. The sweathouse was smaller than a family house. Normally it had a center pole framework with a firepit on the ground next to the pole. When the fire was lit, some smoke was allowed to escape through a hole at the top of the roof; however, most was trapped inside the building. Smoke and heat were the main reasons for having a sweathouse. Both were believed to be a way to purify tribal members' bodies. Sweathouse walls were mainly hard-packed earth. The heat produced was not a steam heat but came from a wood-fed fire.

In the center of most villages was a large house that often had no walls, just a roof held up with poles. It was here that religious dances and rituals were held, or visitors were entertained.

Dances were enjoyed and were performed with great skill. Music, usually only rhythm instruments, accompanied the dances. For some reason California Native Americans did not use drums to create rhythms for their dances. Three different kinds of rattles were used by California tribes.

One type, split-clap sticks, created rhythm for dancing. These were usually a length of cane (a hollow stick) split in half lengthwise for about two-thirds of its length. The part still uncut was tightly wound with cord so it would not split all the way. The stick was held at the tied end in one hand and hit against the palm of the other hand to make its sound.

19

A pebble-filled moth cocoon made rhythm for shaman duties. These could range from calling on spirits to cure illnesses, to performing dances to bring rain. Probably the best sounds to beat rhythm for songs and dances came from bundles of deer hooves tied together on a stick. These rattles have a hollow, warm sound.

The only really "musical" instrument found in California was a flute made of reed that was played by blowing across the edge of one end. Melodies were not played on any of these instruments. Most North American Indians sang their songs rather than playing melodies on music instruments.

Special songs were sung for each event. There were songs for healing sick people, songs for success in hunting, war, or marriage. Women sang acorn-grinding songs and lullabies. Songs were sung in sorrow for the dead and during story-telling times. Group singing, with a leader, was the favorite kind of singing. Most songs were sung by all tribe members, but religious songs had to be sung by a special group. It was important that sacred songs not be changed through the years. If a mistake was made while singing sacred music, the singer could be punished, so only specially trained singers would sing ritual songs.

All songs were very short, some of them only 20 to 30 seconds long. They were made longer by repeating the melodies over and over, or by connecting several songs together. Songs usually told no story, just repeated words or phrases or syllables in patterns.

Song melodies used only one or two notes and harmony was never added. Perhaps that is why mission Indians, at those missions with musician priests, especially loved to sing harmony in the church choirs.

Songs and dances were good methods of passing rich tribal traditions on to the children. It was important to tribal adults that their children understand and love the tribe's heritage.

Children were truly wanted by parents in most tribes and new parents carefully watched their tiny babies day and night, to be sure they stayed warm and dry. Usually a newborn was strapped into a cradle and tied to the mother's back so she could continue to work, yet be near the baby at all times. In some tribes, older children took care of babies of cradle age during the day to give the mother time to do all her work, while grandmothers were often in charge of caring for toddlers.

Children were taught good behavior, traditions, and tribal rules from babyhood, although some tribes were stricter than others. Most of the time parents made their children obey. Young children could be lightly punished, but in many tribes those over six or seven years old were more severely punished if they did not follow the rules.

Just as children do today, Native American youngsters had childhood traditions they followed. For instance, one tribal tradition said that when a baby tooth came out, a child waited until dusk, faced the setting sun and threw the tooth to the west. There is no mention of a generous tooth fairy, however.

Tribal parents were worried that their offspring might not be strong and brave. Some tribes felt one way to make their children stronger was by forcing them to bathe in ice cold water, even in wintertime. Every once in a while, for example, Modoc children were awakened from sleep and taken to a cold lake or stream for a freezing bath.

But if freezing baths at night were hard on young Native Americans, their days were carefree and happy. Children were allowed to play all day, and some tribes felt children did not even have to come to dinner if they didn't want to. In those tribes, children could come to their houses to eat anytime of the day.

The games boys played are not too different from those played today. Swimming, hide and seek among the tule reeds, a form of tetherball with a mud ball tied to a pole, and willow-javelin throwing kept boys busy throughout the day.

Fathers made their sons small bows and arrows, so boys spent much time trying to improve their hunting skills. They practised shooting at frogs or chipmunks. The first animal any boy killed was not touched or eaten by him. Others would carry the kill home to be cooked and eaten by villagers. This tradition taught boys always to share food.

Another hunting tool for boys was a hollowed-out willow branch. This became like a modern day beanshooter, only the Native American boys shot juniper berries instead of beans. Slingshots made good hunting weapons, as well.

Girls and boys shared many games, but girls playing with each other had contests to see who could make a basket the fastest, or they played with dolls made of tule. Together, young boys and girls played a type of ring-around-the-rosie game, climbed mountains, or built mud houses.

As children grew older, the boys followed their fathers and the girls followed their mothers as the adults did their daily work. Children were not trained in the arts of hunting or basketmaking, however, until they became teenagers.

HISTORY

Spanish missionaries, led by Fray Junipero Serra, arrived in California in 1769 to build missions along the coast of California. By 1823, fifty years later, 21 missions had been founded. Almost all of them were very successful, and the Franciscan monks who ran them were proud of how many Native Americans became Christians.

However, all was not as the monks had planned it would be. Native American people had never been around the diseases European white men brought with them. As a result, they had no immunity to such illnesses as measles, small pox, or flu. Too many mission Indians died from white men's diseases.

Historians figure there were 300,000 Native Americans living in California before the missionaries came. The missions show records of 83,000 mission Indians during mission days. By the time the Mexicans took over the missions from the Spanish in 1834, only 20,000 remained alive.

The great California Gold Rush of 1849 was probably another big reason why many of the Native Americans died during that time. White men, staking their claim to tribal lands with gold upon it, thought nothing of killing any California tribesman who tried to keep and protect his territory. Fifty-thousand tribal members died from diseases, bullets, or starvation between the gold Rush Days and 1870. By 1910, only 17,000 California Indians remained.

Although the American government tried to set aside reservations (areas reserved for Native Americans), the land given to the Indians often was not good land. Worse yet, some of the land sacred to tribes, such as burial grounds, was taken over by white people and never given back.

Sadly, mission Indians, when they became Christians, forgot the proud heritage and beliefs they had followed for thousands of years. Many wonderful myths and songs they had passed from one generation to the next, on winter nights so long ago, have been lost forever.

Today some 100,000 people can claim California Native American ancestors, but few pure-blooded tribespeople remain. Our link with the Wanderers, who came from Asia so long ago, has been forever broken.

The bullroarer made a deep, loud sound when whirled above the player's head. Tipai tribe.

Villages were usually built beside a lake, stream, or river. Balsa canoes are on the shore. Tule reeds grow along the edge of the water and are drying on poles on the right side of the picture.

Women preparing food in baskets, sit on tule mats. Tule mats are being tied to the willow pole framework of a house being built by one of the men.

WINTU TRIBE

INTRODUCTION

The word Wintu (Win' tuh) means 'person' in the language of the Wintu tribe's neighbors. Some historians have given this tribe the name Wintun, which has the same meaning as the word Wintu. We shall call it Wintu.

The tribe had two kinds of plant life areas in its territory. One area was the desert-like floor of the Sacramento Valley, along the western side. Plants that needed little water, such as manzanita, grew there. The second type of plant life was found in the higher land, or foothills, of the valley. More trees were found in this area. Oak trees, which produced much-needed acorns, grew in the lower region of the foothills of this area.

Wintu territory included parts of what are now the modern California counties of Shasta, Siskiyou, Tehama and Trinity. The Wintus had more people than any other Northern California tribe, numbering about 26,000. They could be found living in more than 100 villages within their territory.

Wintu tribal members were described as an active, wealthy tribe of people who were looked up to by the ten smaller tribes of Native Americans around them.

THE VILLAGE

From 20 to 250 people lived in a village, which could have from four to thirty-six bark houses in it. Village houses came to a point at the top, like upside-down ice cream cones. These bark homes had a framework of poles, tied together at the top. The poles were covered with bark or with evergreen boughs. Homes higher in the mountains, also cone-shaped, had walls of wood slabs, giving villagers more protection from the cold winters.

Inside the houses were storage baskets containing household belongings, a fire pit, and on the floor, mattresses made of grass, tree boughs, or deerhide.

The sweathouse of this tribe was very large compared to those of other California tribes. It was an earthen lodge built big enough to hold from 50 to 70 people at one time. Most other tribal sweathouses were tiny, some so small men could not stand up inside them.

The sweathouse-earthen lodges were round in shape, and the floor had been dug into the ground several feet. A center pole held up the roof. A smoke hole at the top of the lodge was also used as an entrance. Either notches were cut in the center pole, so it could be climbed, or a ladder was tied to the pole with grapevines.

Ceremonial lodge, cut in half to show inside of the underground lodge.

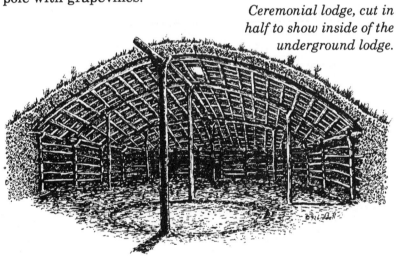

The earthen lodge was a meeting place for men of a village. Many events took place there. Shamans' yearly initiations, and daily sweating, which tribal men felt purified their bodies, took place there. Often unmarried men slept in the lodge during cold weather.

There seems to have been no separate dance house in Wintu villages until the late 1800s, when a religion called The Ghost Dance became popular. Before that time the earthen lodges were used for any religious rituals or dances.

Granaries, placed near houses around the village, held stored acorns gathered in the fall of each year. These were woven somewhat like a basket, and having the look of the outside of a bird nest. The basketry granary was about four feet in diameter, shaped like a tall column, and was kept off the ground by several support posts placed around it.

VILLAGE LIFE

A family's needs were thought to be more important to Wintu tribal members than those needs of its village or tribelet. Village needs were second in importance, and tribelet problems were of little importance.

Villages were led by chiefs who took over the jobs from their fathers. Usually the oldest son would become the new chief when an old one decided to step down. A chief, however, needed to be intelligent, popular with the village people, and a good singer and dancer. If the eldest son could not fill these needs, another son would be chosen.

Village chiefs made most of the major decisions for their villages. They decided when events like dances or meetings would be held, and sent messengers to deliver invitations to feasts they gave. Chiefs handed out punishment to villagers who did not follow tribal laws.

When a villager stole something, and the chief knew who had stolen it, he asked the thief to give back the stolen property. If a thief did not return the property, a chief could order the criminal to be

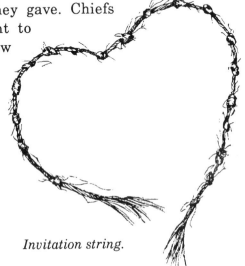

Invitation string.

severely punished. A chief might also take some of the thief's property and give it to his victim.

It was also thought to be good punishment to make fun of a troublemaker in public. Some chiefs even allowed villagers to kill a criminal who had murdered more than once.

Another duty of chiefs was to decide what gifts or repayment should go to families of those people who were killed or hurt in accidents around their own villages. If someone accidentally hurt another villager, gifts, like beads or shells, were paid to the victim's family. In the case of an accidental death of a young man, gifts of from two to five arm lengths of clam disk beads or dentalia had to be paid to his family by the person blamed for the accident.

A Wintu chief did not have to hunt or fish, since a large share of foods gathered or hunted by his villagers belonged to him. Any food a chief had was used to feed not only his family but guests to his village, such as traders. It was also the duty of a chief to feed the village's poor people. No one was allowed to go hungry in a tribal settlement.

Mothers-to-be took very good care of themselves while awaiting the birth of a child. Young women carefully followed certain beliefs in the hope that doing so would make her baby healthy and happy.

One belief was that if she always chewed on a type of grass used in making baskets, the mother-to-be would help her baby's chances of being strong.

Mothers-to-be were also careful never to come face to face with wild animals and not to look too closely at fish, for those things might bring harm to her future baby. To see a bear was especially bad luck for a mother and her coming child. It was also considered bad luck to wear clothes with knots tied in them.

A baby was born in a special birth hut, staying there for a about a month. Then mother and child would leave the birthing hut and return to their family house. The baby was given a new, larger, more carefully made cradle at that time. Usually the cradle had been made by a friend of the new mother.

As a part of the homecoming ritual of a first-born baby, the father handed its newly made cradle to a fast runner. This runner followed a tribal custom of racing completely around the family house with the cradle at least once, before the baby could go into the family home. If the first baby was a girl, a girl runner carried the cradle. A boy runner was chosen to carry the cradle for a baby boy. The baby's other cradle was left hanging in a tree to rot, as a wish for good luck.

After a baby was born, both mother and father put themselves on a special diet of no salt, no meat, and no cold water. This was thought to be a way to make sure their baby would have a good life.

Names were given to a child when it was old enough to understand what the name meant. Relatives, or old villagers, could give a child any name they had a right to give. For instance, through the death of someone related to them, that person's name was their property to give away.

This was important, because saying the name of a dead person aloud was taboo. By giving a dead person's name to another villager, if the name was accidentally said aloud, relatives no longer needed to worry about the taboo.

If living people gave their names to a new baby, then they had to find another name for themselves. That was no problem, however, since most people had two or three names, anyway. Some people had as many as seven names! After the death of parents, a woman usually inherited her mother's name and a man inherited his father's name.

All children were taught the importance of taking many river baths. Parents also took steam baths as examples to their children of the importance of being clean.

Between play times, children learned the teachings of tribal laws and rules. Girls were taught the art of basketmaking and how to prepare and gather food. Boys learned the skills of hunting, fishing, game-playing, and speech-making.

When a boy killed his first deer, or caught his first salmon, his parents gave a feast for villagers. The boy could not eat any of this meat, it all had to be given to others to eat, a good lesson in sharing.

Girls were given a dance in the fall of the year that they became teenagers. Neighboring villagers came and brought food. Each visiting group of people came into the teenagers' village singing. There was dancing and the girls were dressed in new apron-skirts. They carried deer-hoof rattles to beat rhythm for dance performers. This event went on for five days, longer if the food lasted.

Women's front apron of buckskin and pine nuts.

When a villager died, the body was buried the same day. Men took care of the dead body, if the person who died was a man. Women prepared the bodies of dead women. The body was dressed in its best clothes and placed on a doeskin or bearskin hide. This hide was then folded over the body and bound with rope or animal sinew.

A special opening was made in the house's back wall, and the body was taken through this hole to the village cemetery. Cemeteries were found some 300 feet from a village. Graves were dug by several old women of the village. Personal belongings were put in the grave, along with a basket of acorn-meal water for the body's soul to drink.

After a funeral, all those helping with the dead person had to purify themselves by bathing, taking a sweat bath, or by sitting in the smoke of a scrub-oak, live-oak, or fir fire.

Mourners grieved for about one year. During that period of time the widow cut off her hair, rubbed tree pitch into her head, and smeared her face with a mixture of charcoal and pitch. A powder of burned, crushed clamshells was poured over the charcoal and pitch to keep the skin from being too sticky.

WAR

A village chief was in charge of settling any problems which arose between his village and other villages and tribes. Most problems were with nearby villages, often because hunters trespassed onto neighboring territory while hunting. Since most people were related in some way to another village's people, open war was not fought too often.

Weapons used for war were bows and arrows, clubs, thrusting spears, daggers, and slingshots. Elkskin was made into chest armor because of the toughness of its hide. Wooden pole armor was also worn as a vest. Hand to hand fighting was not fought, if at all possible.

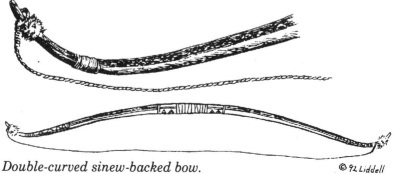

Double-curved sinew-backed bow.   © 92 Liddell

In a battle, two lines of warriors faced each other and exchanged arrow shots until one or another of the chiefs called a halt. The winning side was allowed to take whatever valuables there were on the battlefield. A chief always got the best part of valuables, or loot, of any battle.

At the end of a war, messengers were sent to war leaders of the losing enemy villages, or tribes, telling them where to meet to discuss terms of peace. A chief had already met with his important village men to figure out what the village's terms of peace should be.

All war leaders came to such meetings carrying weapons. Peace agreements with an enemy village included repayment for damage, death, and other losses the sides had suffered. A war dance was performed at the winning village in celebration of a victory.

MUSIC AND GAMES

Other dances performed by Wintu tribelets were more for social, rather than for religious reasons or to celebrate a victory. Dances were celebrated after pine nut and clover harvests each year. There were dances given after salmon runs, rabbit and quail snarings, deer and bear hunts, and after the burnings to capture grasshoppers. Songs, both religious and nonreligious, also were a part of village life.

Along with singing and dancing, celebrations included games of all kinds. Games of chance were probably the most popular with tribal members. Dice were made by women of the tribe. They could be made from walnut half shells, filled with tar, and decorated with pieces of abalone shell or beads. The women wove basket trays to use when throwing dice.

Contests of skill and strength, such as foot races, wrestling, jumping, and bow shooting were watched and cheered at big festivals. Hand games were popular, as well. One hand game, called 'big wood,' lasted for 48 hours because of a game rule which said that honorable players had to play as long as someone challenged them.

Women played the outdoor game of shinny, which was a little like our modern game of field hockey. Hoop and pole, a skill game in which players tried to throw a pole through a hoop as it rolled down a hill, was highly popular.

Children played string games. One called 'buzz' is still played by some children today. A piece of bark with a hole in it was threaded with a double string of buckskin. When the strings were twisted and held in both hands the bark caused a humming sound as the hands closed in and spread out. Today we use string threaded through buttons to get the same humming sound.

RELIGION

Wintu tribal members believed in a supreme being above them. They gave this being a name like 'one who is above' or 'the great man.' When a Wintu man went to the river to wash each morning, he prayed and talked to the sun. A prayer was also said, as one faced the sky, before eating meals.

As with other California tribes, the Wintu people felt animals had supernatural powers. A grizzly bear was greatly feared. Some believed that when the reflection of the moon moved across a lake, it was because a grizzly bear was running around the moon.

Thunder and lightning were thought to be twins of Grizzly Bear Woman. Shooting stars were believed to be spirits of shamans who had died. Northern lights were felt to be a sign of illness coming.

Many beliefs came from tribal myths which had been passed down in stories told from generation to generation. The

Wintu tribe's story on the creation of the world tells of humans first being also part animal.

The creation myth told of many worlds before this one, and that this world itself had been destroyed three times. According to the myth, the first time fire destroyed Earth. The second time a cold north wind blew everything away, and the third time it was a flood that destroyed everything. Wintu people felt that the end of our world will come when there are no more Native Americans.

Tribal members could ask for a shaman's power for good luck in games or hunting trips at special holy places built in their village. Caves, whirlpools in a river, and other such places were thought to be where sacred spirits lived. Flat stones, called charmstones, were worn around the neck to protect a villager from sickness or harm.

Shamans were in charge of the spiritual life of villagers. Since they were believed to have supernatural powers which kept them in touch with spirit-gods, they were called when a villager became ill or had an accident.

Shamans had their own magic objects to help them cure a sickness. Many of them used dancing to call to spirits. Others did sleight-of-hand tricks like modern magicians do today, by making pain objects seem to come from the body of a sick person. The object would be any symbol from a snake to a feather or a small pebble. Payment to the shaman was decided upon before the curing but was paid after the cure.

KNOWLEDGE

Wintus divided their days into morning, middle of the afternoon, dusk, evening, and middle of the night. Years were counted by the old men of a tribelet, who used notched sticks, one for each year. These sticks were planted upright in a row. Less often, some old men put pebbles in a basket to keep track of years.

Months were known by what animals were present during that period of time. By watching the northern and southern route of the sun through the years, older village men were able to figure seasons as we do today: spring, summer, fall, and winter.

Tribal members did their counting over 20 by making piles of clam-disk shells, each containing twenty beads. It was possible to count up into the thousands using the Wintu method.

FOOD

Animal meats were important food for the Wintu tribal members. Deer was plentiful and was probably the main animal eaten. There was almost no waste in the use of a deer. Sinew (animal tendons) was saved to be glued onto bows to make them more bendable. Sinew was stretchy like elastic and could also be used as thread in sewing, or in holding moccasins on the feet when tied around the ankles.

Meat from deer could be cooked by roasting strips of it over a fire, or by wrapping it around a clean hot rock, then covering it with hot coals. Away from the village, a whole side might be cooked over an open fire, to keep it from spoiling on the way home.

Sometimes deer meat was steamed by placing water and hot stones with it in a cooking basket. A basket tray could be used as a cover over the basket to keep steam inside until the meat was cooked.

Brown bears were hunted in the fall, when the animals were getting fat to keep themselves alive during their winter hibernation. Bear meat was greasy, so it was eaten right away rather than dried for later meals. There were some Wintu people who never ate bear meat, especially grizzly bear meat.

Smaller animals, like squirrels or rabbits, were cooked by singeing (burning) off their hair and roasting them in beds of hot coals. Even insects made a tasty treat for the Native Americans. Salmon flies were caught as they swarmed along a river edge in April each year. They could be gathered from the ground in early morning, before their wings were strong enough for them to fly.

A whole village would join in catching grasshoppers. Villagers formed a circle and jumped inward toward each other, driving the grasshoppers into the center of the circle. Grass in the circle center was then set afire. When the fire burned itself out, the grasshoppers, all cooked, were ready to be eaten.

Sometimes grasshoppers were boiled, put on trays to dry, and then stored for winter food. Much fish was also stored for winter. It was cut into strips, sun-dried, and stored in a form much like jerky.

Chinook salmon were plentiful in the large rivers from May to October every year. In the winter months there was another salmon run, so salmon could be caught most of the year in Wintu territory. These were large fish, weighing from 20 to 70 pounds each.

Smaller fish were sun-dried and stored in maple leaves, inside a wide basket with a narrow top. Fish caught in the spring run were too oily to dry for storage. It was baked in long pits lined with heated and washed rocks. Strips of fish were laid over the clean, hot rocks, covered with more hot rocks and baked for a few hours.

Fish left over from the meal, since it was not good for storage, was deboned and flaked. Then it was pounded with a pestle, in a mortar, until it was powdered flour. Sometimes dried roe (a fish) and pine nuts were ground up and

Mortar and pestle.

added to the salmon flour. This flour could then be stored for winter. It had good flavor, so it made a great trading product with other tribes, especially for salt and clam-disk money which the Wintu people wanted.

Grasses, seeds, roots, and especially acorns, were part of the Wintu tribe's plant foods. Manzanita berries were found throughout the territory and were made into a soup or cider. Indian potatoes were dug up in May of each year. The soaproot plant was a very useful plant to villagers. Parts of it were eaten for food, the plant's fibers were used for brushes, certain parts of the plant were used as medicine, and paint and glue could also be made from it.

Soaproot brush.

Clover, wild lettuce, nuts like hazelnuts and pine nuts, wild grapes, and sunflower and cotton-flower seeds are just some of the foods that were gathered every year. Herbal plants, such as pennyroyal, Oregon grape, soaproot, and milkweed were gathered to be used as medicine, as well as for food.

Normally, women gathered all plant foods and men killed all the animals; but if a village was traveling to food-gathering campsites, men and women shared jobs.

Acorns, of course, were one of the tribe's most important foods. If a man found a tree full of acorns while wandering in the woods, he was allowed to claim that tree for his family. To mark the tree as his own until the family could strip it, he used a stick marked with his sign, which he placed on the best branch of acorns.

The gathering of acorns was done by a whole family. Men climbed trees and shook down the acorns, or used hooked sticks to shake branches. Women and children picked up fallen acorns and put them in burden baskets, which women carried to the campsite at day's end.

Trees were stripped one at a time. One large tree, or two small trees, made up a full day's work for a family. In the evening everyone shelled acorns collected during that day. A woman was chosen each day to remain at the campsite to turn over acorns drying in the sun. For this she got a share of the amount gathered on that day.

When enough acorns had been gathered, tribal members returned to their village, the women carrying burden baskets full of nuts on their backs. The shelled, dried acorns were stored in bark-lined pits or in above-ground granaries.

One tribelet was known to have spread open a brush with sticks, lined it with evergreen boughs, and then to have placed shelled acorns in the center. The bush was then tied back into its original shape with grapevines. It probably made a fine granary.

The leaching and pounding of acorns is explained on page 12 in Chapter One of this book. Acorn flour was made into soup, mush, or bread. Soup and mush were cooked by placing flour, water, and hot rocks into a cooking basket. The hot stones were tossed about the basket with a wooden paddle until the soup or mush was cooked.

Bread was baked every few weeks in a stone-lined pit. The stones were heated for a whole day before bread dough was put into the pit. After the stones were heated, they were then covered with dirt, leaves, and more stones. A fire was lit on top of all the rocks as the dough was added. It baked all night and in the morning there was a flavorful bread which could be kept for months without spoiling.

HUNTING AND FISHING

Different methods of deer hunting were used, depending upon whether a hunter worked alone or in a group. Group hunts were by invitation only, and they lasted about three days. When several men were hunting together, the first man to hit a deer with an arrow was owner of the animal, no matter who finally killed it. The hunter who was awarded the deer could share his meat by having a feast and inviting his fellow hunters to the party.

Sometimes hunters used snares set up with bark and tied from one tree to another. The snare's noose was suspended from a bent tree. When a deer entered a noose, the snare released the bent tree, capturing the deer.

Another way of killing deer was to have all village women, children, and older people drive deer into a canyon with a narrow opening at one end. Villagers would yell and beat brush at one end, driving the deer through the canyon. Meanwhile, the best hunters waited at the narrow mouth of the canyon, killing deer as they rushed by. Deer could also be driven over a cliff to their death by groups of hunters chasing them. Men butchered a deer right away and passed pieces of meat to the women to divide between different families.

Single hunters usually wore real deerheads on their own heads and stalked a herd of animals. Tribal men learned to move so much like deer that a good hunter could get right up close to an animal they wanted to kill.

Bows and arrows were used to kill deer. It was not good for a bow to be kept strung, for wood kept bent breaks far more easily then straight wood. Since bows took a long time to make and often the special wood needed came in trade from another tribe, it was important to make a bow last as long as possible.

For this reason, a bow was not strung until just before it was used. Fine hunters could string a bow, arm it with an arrow, and shoot with accuracy as they were racing toward their animal target!

A few Wintu hunters enjoyed the thrill of killing bears, which were needed more for their hides than their greasy meat. Black bears were the usual kind killed. Grizzly bears were never eaten by this tribe because grizzlies killed and ate humans. If hunters found a grizzly bear already dead on the ground, they left it alone to rot.

On the evening of a day someone killed a brown bear, a special ceremony took place. The bear's head was laid in front of a singer. People gathered in a circle around the singer, who accompanied himself with split-stick rattles. The singer would then symbolically kill the bear again, telling the story in song. At one place in the song he would strike the bear's head many times to show how it was killed.

Rabbits were hunted by a group of people only three or four times a season. Snares were set for rabbits. Each snare had a hunter holding a club, standing nearby. As fast as rabbits were caught and killed, the snares were reset. Many rabbits could be killed in a short period of time by using this method. Young boys often practiced their bow and arrow skills by hunting rabbits alone.

Quails were caught in nets. Gophers and other small animals could be caught in deadfall traps. These were made of two flat rocks propped apart by a thin piece of acorn. As the animal tried to eat the acorn, the upper rock fell and crushed it.

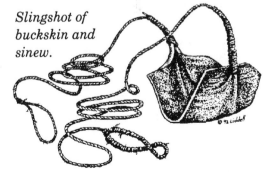

Slingshot of buckskin and sinew.

Squirrels were hunted with slingshots or bows and arrows. Woodrats were hunted in winter, when they did not move as fast as they did in warmer weather. Birds were often hunted by young boys using arrows with only fire-hardened points.

Fish were caught using many different methods. Large fish could be speared with harpoons from small shelters built out over the rivers. Several villages might join together, usually during the summer, to catch a great deal of fish at one time. Any fish caught that way were carefully divided among all villages who had worked together.

Most such fish drives were held in early morning, so the rest of the day could be spent drying fish, feasting, and playing games with people from other tribes. Children who fished on the McCloud River were sometimes given tiny harpoons to spear small fish, as the older men fished for salmon. Women did not join in this type of fishing.

Women would fish in smaller streams, however. Usually weirs (dams of brush weighted down with rocks) were built across creeks and streams to catch fish. Weirs were designed with only one small opening, one or two feet wide, in the middle. A net was stretched across the opening to catch fish as they tried to swim upstream.

Fish hooks were used to catch trout and whitefish. Hooks could be made of anything from two thorns tied together, to a nose bone of deer, or a sharp bird bone. Smaller fish could also be caught in traps.

TOOLS AND UTENSILS

The Wintu people did not inherit a trade (an occupation) from their fathers. Sons were allowed to make their own choices, except for a chief's son. Some men decided to specialize in making bows, or arrows, or nets. For instance, maybe three out of a village of 50 people might be fishermen, making their own nets, traps, or spears. Others might specialize in hunting and making their own bows and arrows. Still others might be best at tanning leather.

A hunter was only as good as his weapons, so much time was taken to make them sturdy and accurate. It took a hunter over six months to make 20 arrows. Arrow shafts were made of cane or reed (hollow wood) with a smaller foreshaft which fit into the larger hollow pocket of the main shaft. At one end of the foreshaft a point of flaked obsidian was attached to it with salmon-skin glue.

When this double-shafted arrow found its target, the foreshaft would remain in the animal, and the main shaft would fall to the ground, so it could be used over and over again.

At the back end of an arrow shaft were three bands of trimmed hawk, or buzzard feathers, called fletching. Usually these feathers were wrapped onto the shaft with sinew. Fletching had to be done exactly right. If the feathers were not placed in proper places on the shaft end, an arrow would not travel in a straight line toward its target.

Not only did the fletching have to be accurate, but arrows had to be straight, as well. Arrow straighteners of grooved stone were used to re-straighten arrow shafts. A crooked arrow was heated over a fire, and then rubbed back and forth in the stone's groove to straighten its shaft.

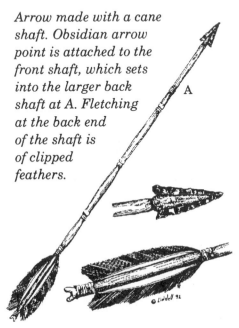

Arrow made with a cane shaft. Obsidian arrow point is attached to the front shaft, which sets into the larger back shaft at A. Fletching at the back end of the shaft is of clipped feathers.

Arrows a man needed for war or hunting were carried in a quiver made of the whole hides of smaller animals, like a fox or mink. Quivers were made with the fur inside and were hung over one shoulder. Each quiver could hold about 40 arrows.

Wintu bowmakers used wood from the yew tree, which they got in trade from another tribe. Wood was allowed to age (dry out) in the shade. Just-cut wood, called green wood, had to be dried out, as it does today, before being made into anything; otherwise it warps or twists.

The back of a bow was strengthened with shredded deer sinew, which was glued on with salmon-skin glue. Since sinew is stretchy animal tendons, this made the bow more bendable. The more bendable a bow was, the farther an arrow could travel toward its target. Bows also were strung with long sinew from a deer's backbone.

Bows were about three feet long and most were decorated with bands of triangles, a Wintu symbol. A special bow, made to kill hibernating bears in their caves, was only about one-and-a-half feet long.

Other weapons village men made were clubs of heavy wood, long daggers made from the front leg bone of a bear, and shorter daggers used only in fighting.

Animal hides were usually tanned to make them softer and more useful. However, brown bear skins were stretched onto a square frame made by the young hunters. The frame was leaned against a tree to let women scrape the inside of the hide with a sharp-edged stone. This was called 'fleshing.' Brown bear skins were used to wrap around dead bodies for burial.

Obsidian hide scraper.

Most other skins were tanned by those village men who were tanning specialists. Deer skins were soaked with deer brains in water. After soaking, the hides were pegged down onto a frame and 'fleshed' with a pumice stone. The skin was then worked between women's hands to further soften it.

Fox skins, and other valuable skins, were not soaked but

fleshed and hand worked. Once in awhile tree moss was rubbed into a hide to color it. Only old women were allowed to help tanning specialists in the early tanning process.

Rope materials took three or four days to gather. Most commonly used was fiber of the iris plant. Women would gather and shred the material but, because strength was needed, men did the actual manufacturing of cord and rope. It took over a week for men to roll and twist fiber into cord long enough for nets and netting.

Fire was carried from place to place smoldering in a white oak branch, or in a small bark bucket with dirt placed under the fire. When a fire had to be started, tribal members used a fire drill set. A set was made up of a flat, hollowed-out piece of cedar and a drill of buckeye oak wood. The drill was spun rapidly back and forth with the hands until sparks caught fire. The drilling set was wrapped in fawnskin until needed.

Mortars, the flat surface upon which seeds and grain were ground, could be a flat rock with a dip in it, or one made from wood. Stone pestles did the grinding and ranged from two inches long, for grinding paint pigments, to three feet long for grinding hard grains.

Awls were used to punch holes while sewing, for flaking obsidian into arrow points, and for weaving baskets. Awls came from animal bones or, better yet, a deer antler. Wedges, needed for splitting wood, were also made from animal horns or antlers.

Sticks used for digging house foundations, or uncovering roots, were made of straightened hardwood, sharpened at both ends. Root digger sticks were from three to four feet long. Those used to dig house foundations and graves were even larger.

Hooked sticks helped pull dead branches down for firewood or were used to make acorn branches reachable. Paddles needed for cooking were made from wood, also. Feathers were not only used as decorations, they also served as paint brushes.

Log rafts were made when streams or rivers had to be crossed and were steered with long poles. Large watertight baskets floated small children and belongings from one side of a river to the other. They were pushed by swimmers or waders, if the water was shallow enough. Sometimes bridges were built across small streams by tying two large poles together with grapevines.

A balsa boat was used for traveling on large lakes. These were made of tightly tied bundles of tule reeds so they would not leak. The balsa boat was narrow with rather high sides. It had a raised bow and was steered with double-sided paddles.

Most baskets made for everyday use by the Wintu tribal women were twined. Young, bendable hazelwood branches, skunkbush twigs, and poison oak (!) stems were used as a base for many Wintu baskets. When a length of branch being woven ran out, the end of the next branch was first chewed by the basketmaker to flatten it before it was overlaid on top of the last branch.

Baskets made by this tribe had a smooth look to them because the weaving material was always twisted to keep a smooth side outward. Some of the most highly prized Wintu baskets were made with porcupine quills.

After a basket was woven, it was soaked in water, shaped, and filled with sand until it had dried into a good shape. Old misshapen baskets could sometimes be reshaped this way.

Ordinarily, twined baskets are more loosely woven than coiled baskets, and they are not as pretty. Coiled baskets were so handsome they were used to hold treasures, given as gifts, or were woven just for trading with other tribes.

Twined burden baskets, used to haul heavy loads on women's backs, were shaped like cones. Basket trays or shovel-shaped trays were needed as flour sifters and sieves, or as dinner plates. Basket hoppers with no bottoms were glued to the tops of stone mortars to keep bits of grain being ground from flying into the air.

Small baskets were used as cooking bowls, eating bowls, or as cups. Large baskets, shaped like bottles, were tightly woven and sealed with tar so they could carry and store water.

Designs woven into the baskets usually had a meaning. One design was a quail crest, another was called an elbow-joint pattern, and one was symbolic of flying geese.

Open twined storage basket.

TRADE

Any extra tools or baskets could be used as products for trading. Native American tribes found they could get things they needed by trading for them. Sometimes items were traded for work done; for instance, if a ropemaker loaned a hunter a long line of rope. When the rope was returned, the hunter who borrowed it could have included a portion of meat he had caught, or an animal hide, in exchange for the use of the rope. Trading between villages and tribelets was done more often than trading between tribes. Trading with other tribes, however, made it possible to own items or products that came from far-distant places.

Shasta Tribe traders offered the much-wanted dentalia shells, along with their best volcanic glass, obsidian. They traded for deer hides and feathered woodpecker scalps which the Wintu tribe had in plenty. Wintus near McCloud River traded salmon flour for the Achumawi tribe's salt. Bald Hills Wintus traded seeds and acorns, plus clam disk money, for McCloud River Wintu salmon.

Whenever obsidian was traded, it was for objects of great value, like bows, arrows, or quivers. If there was something a tribal member wanted, but had nothing of equal value with which to trade, then string money was offered.

Clam-disk money was made of small disk beads strung onto a fiber string. Unlike almost every other California tribe, the Wintu traders did not measure the length of string money around their fists to figure its value. Instead, they counted the number of beads on a string, using multiples of twenty.

The most valuable properties a Wintu could own included bows and arrows, clam-disk money, skins of such animals as otter and fox, mountain woodpecker scalps, obsidian knives and spears with obsidian tips. To own these things, a Wintu trader would pay most of his money or exchange most of his belongings.

CLOTHING

Women always wore skirts of fabric made from the shredded inner- bark of a maple tree. Most skirts hung down from the waist to just below the knees. On special occasions women wore a doe- or fawnskin, fringed-hem apron over the front of their skirts. Feather down (fluffy bird feathers) netted caps were worn on their heads during special events, as well. A deerskin cape, usually made of a whole deer hide, was worn by both men and women in cooler weather.

Women also wore twined basket caps on their heads, especially when they carried heavy burden baskets on their backs. A netting tumpline attached to a basket on one side, came across the woman's forehead and down to the basket's opposite side. The cap helped keep pressure of a heavy load off her forehead.

Men went naked or wore buckskin breechcloths, held at the waist with a belt made of human hair or porcupine quills. Men often tied a netting around their waists to carry their belongings. Their hair was often rolled into knots at the tops of their heads. If they owned daggers, the daggers were tucked into hair knots so they were always handy.

Young girls kept their hair cut in bangs to cover their foreheads. The bangs were allowed to grow out when they married. Smaller children seldom wore clothing, unless the weather was cold.

Cold weather meant that adults wore capes of sewn-together rabbit skins around their shoulders. These long capes were actually blankets used for sleeping at night.

For decorations, women wore earrings of shell or bone in their pierced ears. Piercing was done with a porcupine quill when the girls were quite young. Women also had tattoos cut into their skins with the sharp edge of an obsidian blade, usually when they became teenagers. Most tattoo designs were put on their chins. Wintu girls had three lines running straight down the chin, probably to show to which family they belonged.

After the skin cuts were made, a mixture of pitch and soot was rubbed into the fresh cuts. If a blue-green tattoo was wanted, a certain grass or spider web, was put into the mixture instead of tree pitch.

Wintu men never wore tattoos. For dances, however, they dressed up in fancy costumes of feather skirts and headdresses, capes, and headbands made from yellowhammer bird feathers. Strips of otter, mink, and fox fur, and sometimes the white fur from a fox's stomach, were made into costume decorations. Like women, the men had pierced ears and some pierced their nose bones. Earrings were worn and if the nose was pierced, small dentalium shells were worn in the nose.

HISTORY

Wintu tribal members did not see white people until around 1826, almost the end of the mission period. Spanish missionaries had founded all 21 California mission by that time. However, the missions were all built close to the coast and Wintu land was far north of Mission Solano, the most northern mission.

Animal trappers from Oregon country were the first to enter Wintu land in 1826. Some of them were ill with malaria. Native Americans had never been around white people's diseases, so they had no body immunity to protect themselves from such things as measles, small pox, and malaria.

The malaria epidemic caused by those trappers is known to have killed 75% of all Wintus who lived around the upper and central Sacramento Valley. By the time white settlers arrived a few years later, most of the Wintu tribal members were dead.

When the settlers came, they brought cattle and sheep with them, which grazed all over Wintu territory. The animals ate all the grasses tribal members needed for seed. The Gold Rush followed in 1849, and unfortunately, gold was discovered on Wintu land. Gold miners overran Wintu property, destroying and polluting their streams and rivers by washing down whole hills in their mad rush to find gold.

In 1850, white settlers gave what they called a friendship feast for Wintu tribal members. Only the "friendship" feast turned out to be a terrible trick on the tribe, for the food had been poisoned. More than 100 Wintus died as a result of the party. Before that Wintu tribelet could warn the rest of its people, 45 more Wintu people died at another 'friendship' feast given by settlers for a neighboring tribelet.

More was to come. In 1851 gold miners burned down a Wintu Council meeting house, killing 300 Native Americans having a meeting inside the house. A small bit of land was given to the Wintus by the United States government, but they could not keep it for very long. Over 1,000 gold miners simply took over the government land grant given to the tribal people. One hundred more Wintu people were killed a short time later. Finally the remaining 300 Wintus were rounded up and placed on government reservations.

The last large gathering, a fish drive, of one Wintu tribelet on traditional land took place in the late 1800s. No more fish drives could be held after that because copper-processing plants were built on the rivers. They destroyed all plant life and polluted the water so badly, the fish were no longer fit to eat.

In the 1930s several dams, including Shasta Dam, were built, flooding all remaining Wintu reservation land. With their land almost entirely under water, the Wintu tribal members had no ancient land left.

Today Wintu people live all over the United States. They work in every kind of job, from professional sports to business and industry. Many own their own homes and businesses. However, Shasta County records show that the largest number of unemployed people, and those with the most health needs, are the Wintu tribal members who still live there.

WINTU TRIBE
OUTLINE

I. Introduction
- A. Meaning of name
- B. Two types of plant life
- C. Population of tribe before explorers
- D. Personality of tribe

II. The village
- A. Number of people in villages
- B. House description
- C. Sweathouse description
- D. Granaries

III. Village life
- A. Village chief
  - 1. How chosen
  - 2. Duties
  - 3. Hunting done for chief
- B. Birth
  - 1. Mother-to-be taboos
  - 2. Birth hut
  - 3. Homecoming ritual
  - 4. Naming of child
- C. Childhood
  - 1. River baths
  - 2. Training in tribal rules and laws
  - 3. Boy's "first kill" feast
- D. Teenage
  - 1. Girls' teenage dance event
- E. Death
  - 1. Burial rituals
  - 2. Mourning rituals

IV. War
- A. Biggest reason for war
- B. Weapons used
- C. The battle
- D. Peacemaking

V. Music and Games
- A. Music
  - 1. Dances
  - 2. Singing
- B. Games
  - 1. Games of chance
  - 2. Outdoor contest
  - 3. Children's games

VI. Religion
- A. Supernatural powers and animals
- B. Myths
  - 1. Creation myth
- C. Shamans
  - 1. Curing rituals

VII. Knowledge
- A. Counting
- B. Seasons and months

VIII. Food
- A. Preparations, cooking, and other uses of animals
- B. Kinds of animals
- C. Insects
- D. Fish
- E. Plants
- F. Nuts
  - 1. Acorns, gathering, storing, preparation, cooking
- G. Pit ovens

IX. Hunting and Fishing
- A. Hunting
  - 1. Group and single hunters
  - 2. Kinds of animals and birds hunted
  - 3. Traps, drives, and snares
- B. Fishing
  - 1. Group and single fishing
  - 2. Methods of fishing
  - 3. Tools used for fishing

X. Tools and utensils
   A. Specializing crafts of tribal men
   B. Weapons
      1. Description of bows and arrows
      2. Other weapon descriptions
   C. Leather tanning
   D. Rope description and uses
   E. Stone tools
   F. Wood tools
   G. Rafts and boats
   H. Baskets
      1. Kinds and descriptions
      2. Designs
XI. Trade
   A. Products
   B. String money
XII. Clothing
   A. Women
   B. Men
   C. Young girls
   D. Warmer clothing
   E. Decorations and ornaments
      1. Tattoos
XIII. History
   A. First contact with white people
   B. Epidemics
   C. Settlers
   D. "Friendship" feasts
   E. Gold miners
   F. White people's damage to Wintu territory
   G. Today

GLOSSARY

AWL: a sharp, pointed tool used for making small holes in leather or wood

CEREMONY: a meeting of people to perform formal rituals for a special reason; like an awards ceremony to hand out trophies to those who earned honors

CHERT: rock which can be chipped off, or flaked, into pieces with sharp edges

COILED: a way of weaving baskets which looks like the basket is made of rope coils woven together

DIAMETER: the length of a straight line through the center of a circle

DOWN: soft, fluffy feathers

DROUGHT: a long period of time without water

DWELLING: a building where people live

FLETCHING: attaching feathers to the back end of an arrow to make the arrow travel in a straight line

GILL NET: a flat net hanging vertically in water to catch fish by their heads and gills

GRANARIES: basket-type storehouses for grains and nuts

HERITAGE: something passed down to people from their long-ago relatives

LEACHING: washing away a bitter taste by pouring water through foods like acorn meal

MORTAR: flat surface of wood or stone used for the grinding of grains or herbs with a pestle

PARCHING: to toast or shrivel with dry heat

PESTLE: a small stone club used to mash, pound, or grind in a mortar

PINOLE: flour made from ground corn

INDIAN RESERVATION: land set aside for Native Americans by the United States government

RITUAL: a ceremony that is always performed the same way

SEINE NET: a net which hangs vertically in the water, encircling and trapping fish when it is pulled together

SHAMAN: tribal religious men or women who use magic to cure illness and speak to spirit-gods

SINEW: stretchy animal tendons

STEATITE: a soft stone (soapstone) mined on Catalina Island by the Gabrielino tribe; used for cooking pots and bowls

TABOO: something a person is forbidden to do

TERRITORY: land owned by someone or by a group of people

TRADITION: the handing down of customs, rituals, and belief, by word of mouth or example, from generation to generation

TREE PITCH: a sticky substance found on evergreen tree bark

TWINING: a method of weaving baskets by twisting fibers, rather than coiling them around a support fiber

NATIVE AMERICAN WORDS
WE KNOW AND USE

PLANTS AND TREES
hickory
pecan
yucca
mesquite
saguaro

ANIMALS
caribou
chipmunk
cougar
jaguar
opossum
moose

STATES
Dakota – friend
Ohio – good river
Minnesota – waters that
  reflect the sky
Oregon – beautiful water
Nebraska – flat water
Arizona
Texas

FOODS
avocado
hominy
maize (corn)
persimmon
tapioca
succotash

GEOGRAPHY
bayou – marshy body of
  water
savannah – grassy plain
pasadena – valley

WEATHER
blizzard
Chinook (warm, dry wind)

FURNITURE
hammock

HOUSE
wigwam
wickiup
tepee
igloo

INVENTIONS
toboggan

BOATS
canoe
kayak

OTHER WORDS
caucus – group meeting
mugwump – loner politician
squaw – woman
papoose – baby

CLOTHING
moccasin
parka
mukluk – slipper
poncho

BIBLIOGRAPHY

Cressman, L. S. *Prehistory of the Far West.* Salt Lake City, Utah: University of Utah Press, 1977.

Geiger, Maynard, O.F.M., Ph.D. *The Indians of Mission Santa Barbara.* Santa Barbara, CA 93105: Franciscan Fathers, 1986.

Heizer, Robert F., volume editor. *Handbook of North American Indians; California, volume 8.* Washington, D.C.: Smithsonian Institute, 1978.

Heizer, Robert F. and Elsasser, Albert B. *The Natural World of the California Indians.* Berkeley and Los Angeles, CA; London, England: University of California Press, 1980.

Heizer, Robert F. and Whipple, M.A.. *The California Indians.* Berkeley and Los Angeles, CA; London, England: University of California Press, 1971.

Heuser, Iva. *California Indians.* PO Box 352, Camino, CA 95709: Sierra Media Systems, 1977.

Macfarlen, Allen and Paulette. *Handbook of American Indian Games.* 31 E. 2nd Street, Mineola, N.Y. 11501: Dover Publications, 1985.

Murphey, Edith Van Allen. *Indian Uses of Native Plants.* 603 W. Perkins Street, Ukiah, CA 95482: Mendocino County Historical Society, © renewal, 1987.

National Geographic Society. *The World of American Indians.* Washington, DC: National Geographic Society reprint, 1989.

Tunis, Edwin. *Indians.* 2231 West 110th Street, Cleveland, OH: The World Publishing Company, 1959.

Credits:
Island Industries, Vashon Island, Washington 98070
Dona McAdam, Mac on the Hill, Seattle, Washington 98109

Acknowledgements:
Kim Walters, Library Director, and Richard Buchen,
Research Librarian, Braun Library, Southwest Museum
Special thanks

TOLOWA
YUROK KAROK
        ACHUMAWI
     SHASTA
HUPA   ATSUGEWI
YUKI   MAIDU-
            KONKOW
WESTERN N.E. POMO
POMO
        PATWIN
S.E. POMO
SOUTHERN LAKE
POMO   MIWOK
COAST
MIWOK
        EASTERN
        MIWOK
  OHLONE
     NORTHERN
     YOKUTS
  OHLONE   FOOTHILL
            YOKUTS
         TUBATULABAL
   SALINAN
        SOUTHERN
        YOKUTS

       CHUMASH

            GABRIELINO
                      CAHUILLA
   ISLAND   JUANEÑO - LUISEÑO
   CHUMASH
      ISLAND
      GABRIELINO   DIEGUENO
                      (IPAI - TIPAI)

Map Art: Dona McAdam

At last, a detailed book on the
Wintu Tribe
written just for students

Mary Null Boulé taught in the California public school system for twenty-five years. Her teaching years made her aware of the acute need for well-researched regional social studies books for elementary school students. This series on the California Native American tribes fills a long-standing need in California education. Ms. Boulé is also author and publisher of *The Missions: California's Heritage.* She is married and the mother of five grown children.

Illustrator Daniel Liddell has been creating artistic replicas of Native American artifacts for several years, and his paintings reflect his own Native American heritage. His paternal grandmother was full-blood Chickasaw.

ISBN: 1-877599-44-1